Dramatic Moments in Worship

Ev Robertson

© Copyright 2001

LifeWay Press

All Rights Reserved

ISBN 0-6330-1737-X

Dewey Decimal Classification: 812

Subject Heading: Religious Drama/Worship-Drama

Printed in the United States of America

Scripture references marked HCSB are from the *Holman Christian Standard Bible*,

© 2000 by Holman Bible Publisher. Used by permission.

Scripture references marked NIV are from the Holy Bible, *New International Version*,

copyright © 1973, 1978, 1984 by International Bible Society. Used by permission.

Hymn Source is *The Baptist Hymnal*, © copyright 1991

Convention Press. Used by permission.

Permission is granted to photocopy this material for

local churches and other Christian organizations

who have purchased a copy of this script book.

Reproduction in any other form and for any other group

that has not purchased this book is strictly prohibited.

Cover Image © Stone

LifeWay Church Resources

a division of LifeWay Christian Resources

of the Southern Baptist Convention

127 Ninth Avenue North

Nashville, Tennessee 37234

Contents

A word from the writer… 4

Foreword 5

Introduction 6

Scripture Index 63

Topical Index 64

SOLO PIECES

God's Amazing Healing Grace (The Leper) **11**

My Wonderful Peace (Woman at the Well). . **13**

Redeemed (Zacchaeus). **15**

The Shepherd **17**

The Visitor. **18**

The Christmas Gift **20**

Forgiven. **22**

Parable of the Word **24**

PANTOMIME

Two Men Went into a Church **26**

My Gift. **29**

SKETCHES

Oh, To Be Like Jesus 31

Angels All Around 34

Cindy's Perfect Christmas 37

Family War 44

CALL TO WORSHIP

Sing To the Lord 47

Light in the Darkness 48

We Are His 49

AUDIENCE PARTICIPATION

When God Calls 50

SCENARIOS

The Game of Life 52

A Christian Responsibility 53

True Love Waits 54

The Lord's Prayer 55

Worship Changes. 56

Prepare to Worship 57

Offering Interrupted 58

Hymn Interrupted 59

Sermon Interrupted. 60

On Mission 61

CHILDREN'S SERMON SCENARIOS

Our Heavenly Father 62

The Missionaries 62

A Wicked Tongue 62

From the writer . . .

Drama has been a part of my life for the past 49 years. It began when I played a pumpkin in the first grade. It don't remember much about that except that it was fun. I remember people watching me — and what I did and said seemed to have some importance. I've performed in or directed at least one drama a year ever since then.

In 1970 God spoke to me one cold February night while walking down a one-track road in Western Scotland. He spoke audibly and the message was very clear. "I want you to serve me with the gifts and talents I've given you." Chills ran up and down my spine. I pinched myself, checked the hedgerows on both sides of the road to be sure no one was there. I don't share that story with everyone, because most wouldn't believe it, and it's not really important to anyone but me. But it is that calling that has driven me for the past 30 plus years to help our churches learn to use drama effectively in the ministry of our Lord.

I am amazed at how God continues to bless my ministry. It is uplifting to see the hundreds and now thousands of others who have been called and have joined me in humble servitude to our Lord and Savior Jesus Christ.

It is also interesting to note that God does not bless those or their work who try to turn the church into a theater so they can perform their art and craft. He blesses only that which honors Him first. Our first commitment is to Him. Then we use what He's given us to serve. It's really that simple. The hard thing is that He asks us to give everything up for Him. For artists, that means we have to give up our art. When we do a wonderful miracle takes place. He then uses our talents in ways we never dreamed possible.

This book is a continuing part of my call. I challenge you to examine your call! Renew your commitment to Him. And let us serve with all our strength until He calls us home.

"Forgetting what is behind and reaching forward
    to what is ahead,
I pursue as my goal the prize promised by God's
    heavenly call in Christ Jesus,"
(Phil. 3:13b–14, HCSB).

Foreword

The material in this book is designed specifically to help those using drama in worship. All of the scripts have been used successfully in worship. That means they've worked before and if used properly should work again. These scripts by no means represent the total spectrum of dramatic materials that can be used in worship. Other forms of drama – like speech choir, readers theater, interpretive movement, puppetry, clowning, etc. – all have their place. This material simply represents some of my personal work. It is my hope you will find it as valuable as I have.

Please feel free to adapt and rewrite any of this material. It is important that drama fit perfectly with the specific worship experience in which it is being used. That means a personalization of dramatic content may be necessary. Change names, places, dialogue, whatever will work better for you and your situation. I once heard a writer say, "Oh, they can change whatever they like. Just don't tell me about it." I really don't feel that way. Let me know about any changes that work for you. I may be able to use them more effectively in the future.

Also, you may be able to use some of the scripts as an outline for other scripts. That's why I included the scenarios *(scene outlines)*. I personally think the most effective use of drama in worship often demands original material be developed to meet the specific need. These scenarios hopefully will give you some ideas from which you can improvise an original text and rehearse it to a performance level. The improvisation approach makes it possible for anyone, with or without writing skills, to develop an original text.

Finally, should you need additional help related to the production of any of these scripts, please contact me by calling Carson-Newman College in Jefferson City, TN. If you need additional scripts contact Christy Haines, Drama Consultant, LifeWay Christian Resources (877) CH-DRAMA. There are many fine writers out there like Matt and Darlene Tullos, Gail Blanton, and literally hundreds of others. They enjoy writing sketches for the local church. Contact Christy or me and we'll help you find the right writer for your needs.

I want to thank my wife Joy for her continuing support and encouragement. Also I want to thank my good friends Paul and Christy Haines, Matt and Darlene Tullos, and the hundreds of others who continue to lift me up with encouragement in this ministry. May God continue to richly bless you all.

Introduction

The world around us is changing so rapidly that it's becoming increasingly difficult for even the most diligent to stay up with all "that's new." The influence of technology permeates our lifestyle. Just a glance at our culture reveals continuing moral decay; decline of the family and family values; an increase in materialism and all that accompanies it; abortion on demand to compensate for "mistakes"; abuse of women and children; and on and on it goes. Each of us are in the center of all this. Many times we'd like to step aside and pretend we're unaffected, but the truth is none of us can do that. Currently the church faces perhaps the greatest crises since the persecution of the early Christians in Rome. On the outside, the continuing barrages of secular humanism threaten the very existence of religion. On the inside, the church faces major arguments related to biblical authority and interpretation, ordination of women, spiritual immaturity, and worship styles.

The arguments over worship style perhaps touches all of us the most. After all, even when it's corporate in nature, worship is personal in impact. Sunday after Sunday thousands of churches find their fellowship fractured by arguments over the style of music, style of sermon, type of worship space, appropriate musical instruments, and dress of the worshippers. This is really nothing more than a microcosm of what's going on in the world around us. The old is clashing with the new. And the new is changing so quickly it's impossible for the old to catch up. Some have quit trying. "Just do it like we've always done it. That's the best way." That statement is the beginning of the death sentence.

Other churches decide to catch up at all costs. Their drastic changes in worship style destroy community, particularly with older Christians, and make continuity in spiritual growth almost impossible.

Some churches choose to balance precipitously on the fence. "Blended" is their favorite word. The word blended is often a substitute for "bland." But they trudge on, attempting desperately to hold the middle line.

There is another way: God's way. He's revealed Himself to us over and over through our lives. Why not trust Him now? He has a plan for each of us and each of our churches. It is a holy plan and one that is eternal in nature. How can we find that plan? First, we must examine ourselves and our personal relationship to Him. Personal revival and recommitment is mandatory. We don't need to worry about other churches; we need to focus on our church family and what God is revealing to us. We must not allow Satan to distract us with thoughts of, "inadequate resources, not enough people, space, etc." When God gives us a plan, He gives us everything we need to complete the plan. I know that because He does it over and over in my personal life.

Second, we must accept changes in the world around us. We are commanded by scripture to be in the world with the gospel. It is impossible to be in the world if we do not know the language of that world. We must accept the fact that music has undergone and is continuing to undergo major changes in our culture. We must accept the fact that major changes in personal interaction and human communication do affect how we do church, including our preaching.

Third, we must be willing to implement any and all changes that may be necessary for our body of believers to commune with the Lord in corporate worship each Sunday. We make changes not because it's the newest thing, but because it's the appropriate thing.

Drama can be a most effective tool in this process. The basic premise of drama is that it is a "mirror to truth in life." When we use that mirror to see ourselves on a regular basis, our lives are changed. We see our errors and correct them. Jesus did this over and over through His parables. He used the story to show people truth. When used this way drama does not interrupt or disrupt worship. It becomes a tool through which the Lord can enlighten us and help us see Him and each other more clearly.

Best Use of Drama

What are the best ways to use drama? The following are some suggestions.

1. Keep material short in length, to the point, and simple in production style (minimal costumes, props, scenery, and lighting).

2. Use drama throughout the service where it will be most meaningful, not just as a special feature.

3. Use all available space in the worship center, not just the podium. The aisle, choir loft, balcony, even the congregation itself can be used where appropriate.

4. Insure that transitions into and out of the drama are smooth and appropriate for where it's used in the service.

5. Be sure the drama truthfully represents the human experience. It is only through that truth that appropriate spiritual concepts can be applied to help us all.

6. Be sure the congregation can see, hear and understand every word and action of the drama.

7. Use people in the dramatic roles who have the spiritual maturity to be worship leaders.

8. Select a style of drama that will best fit the place it's being used in the service and the message it carries. Avoid using only sketches, or readings, or pantomime, or any other single style. Fit the style to the need.

9. Keep the pastor and other appropriate worship leaders up-to-date on what is being done and how it will be presented so that they can be more effective in their use of it.

10. Continually seek divine guidance throughout the preparation and presentation process.

Applications of Drama

The following are some specific applications of drama.

1. Use drama to enhance any part of worship that may have lost its fervor. For example, many churches take the offering for granted. The spiritual concept of sacrifice has been completely lost in the ritualistic offertory process. Use drama to call attention to the true meaning of the offering. Another glaring weakness in worship today is a lack of "holiness" both in preparation and process. Use drama before services to help the congregation appropriately prepare for worship. Pantomime is silent and an excellent way to use the universal language of gesture to express simple attitudes of "holiness."

2. Use drama to support and expand the biblical revelation through worship. Use it with Scripture reading when it can help bring Scripture to life in a new and meaningful way. It is a wonderful tool for any pastor to use in introducing or illustrating a sermon. It adds a dimension that is impossible for the pastor alone to achieve. It can support by illustrating and introducing music throughout the service. The recent popularity of interpretive movement makes that medium a potentially beautiful illustration of a musical line or thought.

3. Use drama to interpret or bring up-to-date the obscure, or the forgotten basis of certain concepts. For example some hymns still have a contemporary feel, but have words or ideas we no longer use or understand. Terms like "sea billows roll" are completely foreign to many younger people today. Use drama to show the meaning either before, or in some cases, during the hymn. The traditional rituals surrounding the observance of the Lord's Supper have made it ineffective for many today. Use drama to show why each part of the observance is important. During the actual observance, a brief 20-30 second statement by disciples who were at the supper may bring new meaning.

Forms of Drama

What forms of drama are best to use? Here is a list of major forms and suggestions for how to use them.

Sketches: Short, hard-hitting sketches are perhaps the most effective form of drama to use. These brief dialogues take human situations, immediately identifiable by everyone, and express the problems in those situations. Sketches are ideal when joined with the sermon, but also can be used throughout worship.

Pantomime: Silent expression provides a strong visual stimulus lacking in many churches today. It is most effective with controversial, divisive, or material of a highly personal nature. Pantomime requires extreme clarity and simplicity in gesture. The performance time should be brief, rarely exceeding two minutes in length.

Solo Pieces: These seem to work best when they function as testimonies. A person, biblical or modern, can take his situation and explain it to us in simple human terms. These are ideal to illustrate or introduce the sermon and music. They may interrupt at times and jar us into the significance of the moment. For example, a character interrupting the offering with an impassioned personal statement on the true meaning of the offering can bring new significance to it for the entire congregation.

Speech Choir: Using several people to speak a passage of scripture or other written material can provide variety and contrast in the presentation. Three to five voices are ideal for special interpretations of scripture. Use special sound to undergird the presentations (music, sound effects, etc.). It is ideal for the scripture reading.

Interpretive Movement: This is not to be confused with liturgical dance. Interpretive movement can take music and/or scripture and express it in a beautiful contemporary style. Sometimes the pieces are almost like music videos. They can also be highly stylized, not unlike dance, with broad moves which are beautiful to watch and very expressive. They are ideal with special music, and can be used with some scripture readings.

Introduction

Readers Theater: The process of reading a script instead of acting it out can be effective. In fact, some scripts are better performed this way. It is important that some movement be incorporated with the readings to keep them active. Contrasts in voices, sound effects, and staging are critical. It is best used with special features like a mission emphasis, stewardship, or a call to worship.

Puppetry: Puppets continue to be popular due to the high visibility of caricature on television and in the media. Puppets can speak as strongly to adults as they do children. Short, brief dialogues can cover any subject. They are particularly good at dealing with sensitive material like personal stewardship, racial relationships, and similar themes. They are best used during the children's sermon, but can be used any place in the worship service.

Clowning: Some clowns don't want to admit it, but clowning is and always has been a part of the dramatic arts. The development of the American circus clown is only one part in a long and storied history. The clown is similar to the puppet in that he can handle extremely sensitive material. The clown presents a "larger than life" figure that is dealing with human trauma. And he usually presents this in a light-hearted and beautiful way. We see ourselves in the clown, smile, and try to do better in our lives. Clowns can be used any place in the worship experience. They are most effective with children's sermons and in support of special emphases.

Audience Participation: This new form of theater has great potential for use in worship. Verbal and physical congregation responses are illustrated by the piece, *When God Calls*. Responsive movement to music, scripture, and story is also growing in popularity in worship.

Dramatic Improvisation: This proven form of drama continues to offer the best method of quickly developing worship scripts for performance. The scenario section in this book offers good examples of script outlines which can be improvised into scripts by actors, and then rehearsed for performance.

There are many other forms of drama including one-act plays, full-length plays, pageants, and musical dramas. But none of these are really appropriate in the regular worship experience. However they can be extremely worshipful and powerful special presentations of the gospel truth.

Solo Pieces

God's Amazing Healing Grace

The Leper should be performed with great energy – including quick moves and perhaps even running at times. *Leper* enters ringing a small bell.

"Unclean, unclean" – *(to someone on podium)* Hey, I said "unclean." *(rings bell)* "Unclean – unclean," I just love doing this – "Unclean." *(points to someone on podium or in congregation)* Oh, look, he's unclean. *(laughs, rings bell)* "Unclean"– what's that? I don't look unclean? That's right – not a bit of leprosy here – all gone – every bit of it. Oh you think I'm tetched *(points to his head)* Well, maybe I am. You'd be tetched too if someone took your leprosy and *psssst*, just like that, jerked if off of you. Let me tell you about it. See, some of my buddies and I always went into the village on Thursdays to get some vittles for our little clan in the hills. This particular Thursday we were moseying through the market and all of a sudden a big crowd of people rushed by on the street. Well, being the inquisitive sort, I yelled at one of them. "Hey, where all you folks headin' out to?" One of them yelled back, "We're going to see Jesus,

he's just outside of town!" Well now, I'd heard about Jesus – I'd heard he could heal people. *(looks at hands)* Shucks, I knew no man on this earth could heal my leprosy – I'd had it all my life. But it would be interesting to see what this religious man could do. So, I just joined the crowd. When we got out of town there was this big mob of people. I couldn't even *see* Jesus. So, I took out my little bell and let out a little . . . *(rings bell)* "Unclean."

They parted just like the Red Sea and I went right through the middle of them to the center. When I got there Jesus was talking to someone on the other side. I yelled, "Hey, Jesus, you could heal me if you're willing," and I fell on my knees. He looked at me and had a big smile on His face – He walked straight up to me and touched me with his finger right here *(points to center of forehead)*. And that's when it happened. I can't even

Solo Pieces: God's Amazing Healing Grace

Solo Pieces

explain it to you. Something came over me from the tip of my toes to the top of my head. I looked at my hands and the leprosy was gone – I looked at my arms – all gone – felt my face – all gone – it was a miracle. "Hey, look everybody, I've been healed, I've been healed, I've been healed." People cheered and clapped and shouted. It was the biggest commotion you've ever seen. I rolled around in the dust, I was so happy. I ran through the whole crowd yelling – "I'm clean, I'm clean. See, I'm clean." Well, the next thing I knew I was on the back side of the crowd again. That's when I remembered what my mother used to say to me, "Son, if someone does something good for you, you need to say thank you." Well, there wasn't any way I could get back through the crowd. So . . . I took my little bell and let out a loud *(rings bell)* "UNCLEAN!" Just like before, the path was clear, straight to Jesus. When I got to Him I fell on my knees and said, "Thank you Jesus, thank you for healing me." And that's when the second miracle happened that day. Jesus looked at me

and He wasn't smiling this time. His eyes looked down inside me and He saw all that dirty stuff in there – I saw it too and all I wanted was to get rid of it. "Jesus, Jesus, I'm so sorry – will you get rid of all this stuff for me?" And *psst*, just like that, He jerked it out! I was clean, inside and out! And that's when the third miracle happened that day. When I got to my feet, there was a power in me I can't explain. All I wanted to do was go everywhere and tell everybody about Jesus. And that's just what I've been doing. When they won't listen, I just take out my bell and yell *(rings bell)* "Unclean." They think I'm crazy but they'll listen to my story. How about you friend? Are you clean inside and out? Have you been healed? He'll clean you too, just like that *(snaps fingers)*. All you have to do is ask Him! *(rings bell)* "Unclean." *(exits ringing bell and repeating "unclean")*

_____

© Copyright 2001 LifeWay Press
Adapted from the piece that appeared in the Summer 2000 issue of *Church Musician*, LifeWay Christian Resources.

Solo Pieces

My Wonderful Peace

Actress speaks as the Woman at the Well.

Do you know what it's like to seek love and never find it? To desperately want the good things of life and always seem to get the bad? I thought that's the way life was. Get the best husband, live in the biggest house. Those were the goals. I tried different husbands – lived in a big house and never could quite make it! Other women talked about me. They called me lots of names. That's why I learned to live alone – within myself.

Then one afternoon, I went to the well at my usual time – the hottest part of the day. I knew no one else would be there to smirk, to make remarks. He was sitting there – one of them – a Jew. I hurried to draw water – if I was seen with a Jew – I'd never live it down – not in our village – everybody knows everything about everybody.

He spoke to me, "Lady, give me a drink of water." "Since when does a Jew drink from a Samaritan cup," I shot back. "If you ask, I will give you living water!" he replied. I was puzzled – how could he give me water? He had nothing to draw it with. "The water I give is not from this well, it will flow within you forever, an eternal spring."

Solo Pieces: My Wonderful Peace   *Dramatic Moments in Worship* [13]

Solo Pieces

Suddenly chills ran up and down my spine. His words struck me like thunderbolts. "You have five husbands, and the man you live with now is not your husband," he said. Then, His eyes looked deep inside me and He said, "You have always read that God's messenger will make everything clear to you – I am that messenger."

I knew it was true, He was the promised one! Tears of joy filled my eyes – I cannot remember what I said, but I know what I felt and what I did. I was filled with the gentle breeze of peace. Somehow I felt cleansed, and I raced to tell everyone in the village. It didn't matter what they thought, or what they did. I had to tell them – I had to tell them about the man I had met!

That excitement continues to this day – His water of peace fills my life daily, and it never runs dry. My desire for you is that you too could discover my peace – my wonderful peace.

© Copyright 2001 LifeWay Press

Solo Pieces

Redeemed

**Zacchaeus enters flipping a quarter.
The suggestion of a Jewish accent will
add to the effectiveness of the character.**

Twenty-five cents! *(shows congregation)* Not much money to
most people, but this quarter is very important to me. The
name's Zacchaeus. A tax collector. Well known among my
countrymen. Hated, feared. A wretched man to all who knew
me then. Ridiculed in public gatherings, avoided on the street.
And lonely, very lonely! Starved for any companionship, that
was me. Not so unusual among men I'm discovering. How
about you? Any of the terms I've just mentioned ring a
bell? Here I stand before you, flipping a quarter, may I add,
proudly flipping this quarter. It's my most valuable asset – ah,
correction, my second most valuable asset! The first is *(smiles
broadly)* . . . What would you do if you were me? Hide? Close
yourself off in you house? In my case a rather large house on
the most prominent hill in town! What would you do? I hid,
frankly. I appeared only to collect what was due the Governor
and me — usually with soldiers to assist, for as you know, people don't pay taxes without a battle. I hid as long as I could and
then there arrived that fateful day . . . how can I describe it? A
rather common day to most! Bright sunlight, a mainstay where
I live. It was spring and the air was a bit crisp. The kind of day
that sucks one out of a musty house and a dingy existence. I
found myself on the street, breathing the fresh air, smelling the
flowers in bloom, listening to the birds chirping a message of

Solo Pieces: Redeemed   *Dramatic Moments in Worship* [15]

Solo Pieces

new life and hope. Alone. In the midst of that beauty I was alone. People crossed the street to pass on the other side and avoid me. I gazed down the street and I remember the dust. A large cloud floating from the far end. Either a major fight in the street, or a large crowd – perhaps both – following something or someone. I could not quite make it out. The small sycamore tree nearby was perfect for my needs. I quickly climbed it to see over people rushing in front of me toward the cloud. Suddenly He was there, looking straight up at me! Eyes that pierced my soul. His voice shook me from my daze! "Zacchaeus, come down. I dine at your house today!" A vicious murmur spread through the crowd. The Man appeared quite common, and yet he was clearly the focus of the crowd. My house. Dinner. Words no man ever spoke to Zacchaeus. *(pause – tears or the suggestion of tears)* In an instant I felt His warmth inside me. His love permeated my being, shattering the glass I had molded to protect me from a vicious world. We walked side by side the few quick blocks to my house. No one ever walked with me before, but He did. And He stands here beside me today! Right there! Don't you see Him? He's watching me flip my quarter and smiling! For you see, this quarter is the first quarter I ever collected. It reminds me of who I was, and who I am, and who I will always be! *(smiles, slowly flips coin as he turns and exits)*

© Copyright 2001 LifeWay Press

[16] Dramatic Moments in Worship

Solo Pieces: Redeemed

Solo Pieces

The Shepherd

softly humming a hymn or chorus as he gently caresses a small lamb

Ah, my sweet one. A bit too frisky weren't you? Does the leg hurt? It will be well soon and you can once again jump and play. Why, my little one? Why did you want to leave the flock? Why did you move close to the edge of the cliff? To look over it? To jump? Were you drawn to the beauty of the sky that seems to go on forever when you go near the edge? Were you attracted to the taller grass at the edge? My little one . . . why do you think the grass is taller there? Because my sheep know there is danger and they leave it alone. Why did you not leave it alone? Was it doing something different? The adventure? Did that attract you? You are much better off, my little one, to have a small break in your leg. It has saved you from the edge. From moving a bit too close and slipping and falling and . . . I know it hurts. But you are safe! And soon, very soon, the pain will leave. . . the leg will strengthen . . . and you will grow strong! With strength will come wisdom! And with wisdom will come

power to look away from the tall grass. You will move away from the beautiful green grass because you know the edge is near. As you move, others will follow. Your strength will encourage them, and our little flock will grow. And you, my sweet one will remain close to me, very close! I am counting on you! Don't you see? Were you not in my flock you could have slipped, but you are mine. I will protect you and care for you. And yes, it was I who broke your leg with my staff, because you are mine, and I love you. I will always love you and care for you and protect you! And in the future, when you are tempted to move away, it is my strength that will hold you. Oh, you will be tempted from time to time You are a sheep my little one. All sheep like tall green grass, but now you are my sheep. I will always be here to gently pull you back . . . always my sweet one . . . always!

_____

© Copyright 2001 LifeWay Press

Solo Pieces: The Shepherd

Solo Pieces

The Visitor

Just before the worship service begins, a man, dressed business casual, enters the back of the church and walks down the aisle. As he progresses slowly, he looks all around as if in the building for the first time. He observes any adornments that may be present in the room: chandeliers, stained glass windows, beautifully finished pews, nice carpet, etc. He speaks softly at first, as if talking to himself, then gradually gets louder as he notices people are looking at him. He begins to project so that all can hear him.

Man: Beautiful, simply beautiful, excuse me, I don't mean to interrupt anything! What time do you start your meeting? *(to a man sitting on the end of a pew)* Excuse me sir, what time do you start your meeting?

Worshipper: Ah, 10:45!

Man: Well excuse me everyone, I don't want to interrupt your meeting, but you see, ah, ah – my name's Joe Johnson. I live two blocks down from your church. You'll have to excuse me, I've never been in a church before. My folks never went to church and I've never had occasion to come myself. But, you see, all these years I've been watching you come to church, every Sunday. Why in the summer, most folks go to the lake or the beach, but I always see you coming to church. In the winter sometimes the roads are almost impassable and I see you coming to church. All these years . . . I've been wondering . . . why you do it! You're always dressed so nice. And some of you I've watched since you were this tall *(holds hand out)* and now you're

[18] Dramatic Moments in Worship

Solo Pieces: The Visitor

Solo Pieces

grown up. And today, well, I finally built up the nerve to come down here and find out. Like I said, I don't want to interrupt anything, but my curiosity just got the best of me, so I'm here. If it's alright with you I'd like to sit in the back and watch your meeting. If you get to private business or anything, you just say, "Joe, you need to leave now and I'll slip out real quick." You know – years ago on Sunday evenings I used to hear your singing. I have to tell you – it was really uplifting, especially when things weren't going so well. I could sit on my porch, listen to your singing, and somehow I always felt better. I guess since you got the air conditioning in and the windows are shut, the sound doesn't get out like it used to. I don't mind telling you, I miss it. I've been hoping sometime some of you would stop and chat on your way to church. By the way, if you ever want to come by, I've always got the pot on. Just knock and say, "Joe, we're from the church and we've come by to chat a bit." I don't think any of you've ever been by, but it would be nice. I get really lonely sometimes. Well, I guess it's about time for you to start. I'll just take a seat in the back. I just wonder, why are you here today? Why do you come every Sunday? What do you expect to happen in this beautiful place at 10:45 on Sunday morning? *(takes a seat near the rear of the auditorium)*

NOTE: For maximum affect, invite someone from another church who is unknown to your people to come and perform this selection.

© Copyright 2001 LifeWay Press

Solo Pieces: The Visitor

Solo Pieces

The Christmas Gift

Actor enters in clothes of Christmas color and style. Battery-operated Christmas tree lights are strung around his clothes. The lights are not blinking, unless wired so that the actor can cause them to blink and then stop. A few green sprouts stick from pockets. Actor enters humming a Christmas song, secular.

It's almost here! This is my special time. My friends in the forest stood tall and straight as the people came through selecting the "special ones". All my friends said it was an honor to be selected. Those picked would be worshipped, they said. People would hang beautiful ornaments from our branches. String colorful lights around us. Stack beautifully wrapped packages under us. Children, even adults would bow before us as they viewed the packages.

It is an honor, a special honor, or so I've been told. The chosen few will bring laughter and joy to people and children. But, I wonder. I've been standing here in the corner of the Jackson's *(select a last name not in the congregation)* living room for oh, about two weeks now. I'm thirsty. I've discovered something they didn't tell me in the forest. I'm dying. Slowly dying. For what reason? Is the joy I will hopefully bring to this family worth it? Christmas you humans call it. What is Christmas? As I die will the color on the boxes beneath me fade? Will the bright lights dim? Will the ornaments crack? What will happen when the strength of my limbs can no longer hold them? I can't help wondering why! Why must I die for this? Why must I suffer a thirst that cannot be quenched and die?

transition

Solo Pieces

When I walked out here today with my lights blinking, and the twigs sticking from my pockets, some of you smiled. You thought it was funny! A man dressed like a tree! My lights are not blinking now. I can assure you I'm not smiling. There is really nothing funny about this. Oh, some of you are still making fun of me in your hearts. Ridiculous you say. Absurd. Irreverent. Perhaps you would have liked it better if I'd just brought a book and read the story to you. It would be easier that way. No pain. Death could be imaginary, not real! Your conscience would be eased. You're the ones who place me in your houses. You're the ones who dress me up and make me colorful, even beautiful.

transition

Don't worry, I'll be gone from here soon. You can forget Me and all I stand for, at least, for a while. I'll be back! Next year! Once again you'll hang your ornaments, string your lights, wrap your boxes! Will you remember — why? Will you remember death and sacrifice to bring joy and peace? I give My life to you, will you take it? I give My life that you may have a new life. And I will return again, and again, and again. Each time to offer a new start, a new hope. You might even say My image will always be here in this corner for you to see and feel and know…

Actor begins humming again, this time it is *Jesus Paid it All*. He hums as he exits, while a voiceover speaks the words of the chorus to *Jesus Paid It All*, No. 134, The Baptist Hymnal, 1991, Convention Press.

©️ Copyright 2001 LifeWay Press

Solo Pieces: The Christmas Gift

Solo Pieces

Forgiven

The following selection was first performed internally in a sermon,
however, it also can be used to introduce the message.

Man: I know what it means to be forgiven. For me, it all started very
innocently! Some of you know I play tennis every Thursday
mornings at the racket club. Been doing it for years. My
partner's a fellow business associate and he plays about like me,
at best mediocre. For several months two young ladies played at
the same time on the court next to us. We spoke to them occa-
sionally, just strangers making conversation. Then came that
fateful Thursday when my partner didn't show. Her partner
didn't show either and so we decided to play a match! That
started what evolved into a wrong kind of relationship. I didn't
mean for it to happen! I promise you! It was the furthest thing
from my mind. I have a lovely wife, two children. I didn't need
it, didn't want it to happen, but it did. My business friend had
a lengthy illness and had to quit playing. So *we* began to play
together, every Thursday. She was young, she was different, I
don't mind telling you, she got my blood pumping! After a while
there was lunch after our match. Later came afternoon walks
after lunch. And the first thing I knew, all I was thinking about
was seeing her. I made excuses to my wife about working late,
being out of town on business, you name it, I did it. Anything
to be with her. Gradually, I begin to accept the fact that what
we were doing was wrong. When I shared that with her she
expressed the same sentiment. We decided to break it off, and
did. I don't have to tell you how hard I prayed for forgiveness!

[22] Dramatic Moments in Worship

Solo Pieces: Forgiven

Solo Pieces

And my wife? Eventually I told her, and she forgave me! What a joyous day that was. But the most important thing is that He forgave me. The Big Man Upstairs. He filled me with the most wonderful peace! Some of you here this morning may be in the same situation I was in. I have good news! He will forgive you! All you have to do is end that wrong relationship and ask Him. You can do it right now as I lead us in prayer. *(kneeling)* "Oh, Lord. All of us here today are sinners. But we know Father, that you can forgive any and all sin. That's why you sent Jesus, Your only Son to die on that cross. His death buried our sin, and His resurrection brought us new life! Oh Lord! Grant us new life. In Jesus name I pray, Amen!"

At this point, a young girl or boy 6-9 years of age, stands by the man with his/her hand on his head. He/she sings the children's song, "Oh be carefu little eyes what you see. Oh be careful little eyes what you see. For the Father up above is looking down in love. Oh be careful little eyes what you see." Other verses may be sung as appropriate.

———

© Copyright 2001 LifeWay Press

Solo Pieces: Forgiven

Solo Pieces

The Parable of the Wood

**The following piece may be acted out by one or more actors.
It is recommended that at least one actor play the Craftsman.
The crucifixion can be completely pantomimed
and may be timed to the story if you choose.**

Once there was a tree in the forest – a tall, stately, majestic tree. The trees branches towered high, reaching far into the heavens. One day a Craftsman came into the forest, seeking the highest grade of wood to be carved by a great artist. His gaze passed young and old trees searching the depths of the forest. Finally His eyes settled on the tall, powerful tree standing proudly in the center of the woods. He approached the tree carefully, even reverently to begin his task. There was something holy about His chosen target and there was a sadness in His heart as the first stroke fell. For, beneath the fire of His ax was death for this magnificent specimen. The Craftsman knew however that from death He would mold many wondrous works. Gradually, blow by blow, the tree yielded up its last signs of life. Death was swift as the tree plunged to the ground.

Time went by and the wood of the great tree aged under the careful eye of the Craftsman. Finally, it was ready and the Craftsman began His work. The Craftsman's knife began to gently carve away colorful, rich splinters from the wood. A beautiful bowl emerged that would carry the fruit of the vine. Elegant goblets followed that would quench the thirst of a chosen band of men, forever. The knife whittled away and other objects appeared, each designed for a special purpose. With the wood that was left came cruder objects; a frame for a stable, a simple food trough to be placed within, and two large beams, one slightly longer.

[24] Dramatic Moments in Worship　　　　*Solo Pieces: The Parable of the Wood*

Solo Pieces

Time passed and the carvings weathered. Then one star-filled evening a glorious prism of light filled the little stable and new life rushed in The great Craftsman's work was beautiful. Into the special carving of His creation He placed a child, His only Son – the supreme gift of love.

A few years later the Craftsman's tears filled the goblets of twelve men who listened to words like *love* and *serve* and *follow*. The men were drawn in, breathlessly close to the Craftsman's Bread of Life. The Craftsman wept as His Bread was broken under the steel of a soldier's sledge. The Bread was nailed to the final two pieces of the Craftsman's work and raised high in the air; a cross of suffering for all to see. The Craftsman's tears turned red as they flowed through the wood into the crevices of man, cleansing forever all that they touched. And still, the Craftsman's work was not complete.

Three days later the Craftsman's supreme gift of love tore from the shackles of death. New life began and in the center of the forest a new seed was planted. The seed pointed its trunk high into the sky, spreading its branches of love to shelter eternally all who choose to slip under its cover. And there in the center of the forest the Tree of Life stands – its branches of love forever encouraging and protecting, a glimmering beacon high above all other trees. And in the distance the great Craftsman waits – to step into the forest yet a second time and take what is His to its eternal home.

© Copyright 2001 LifeWay Press

Pantomime

Two Men Went into a Church...

May be performed by two men, two women, or combination.

The following action takes place in pantomime with backup piano or other instrument and/or tape. The actors move in rhythm to the music and are very animated. Organ could play first man's theme and piano second man's theme. In any case, one instrument should be more formal and the other freer and less formal. All action is covered by music.

Minister or offstage voice: Two men went into a church.

The formal instrument begins playing "Pomp and Circumstance" *(or a similar piece)*. **Actor 1** enters stage left *(to the congregation's right)* with a hymnal and large Bible in his right hand. He marches with an arrogant attitude to the tempo of the music. This may include looking down on other people on the podium. He places the books on the pulpit, turns to the audience and pulls a written note from his pocket. He faces the congregation, closes eyes, raises one hand, then opens eyes and begins to mime reading fervently from the paper. He freezes. Music stops.

A second instrument begins to play "The Old Rugged Cross" or a similar piece. **Actor 2** enters stage right with his head bowed. He moves to the pulpit, but does not go behind it. He looks at his hands and then raises them to his face in a gesture

[26] *Dramatic Moments in Worship*   *Pantomime: Two Men Went into a Church...*

Pantomime

indicating shame and anguish. He freezes. Music stops.

First instrument begins to play "Pomp and Circumstance," again as **Actor 1** breaks freeze, puts paper in his pocket. He notices the **Actor 2** and moves toward him. He observes the second man, then turns away in disgust. He grabs the hymnal and begins to mime directing music with a very pompous attitude. He freezes. Music stops.

"The Old Rugged Cross" begins to play again as **Actor 2** breaks his freeze. He begins shaking as if weeping – falls to knees. He continues to indicate a deep and troubling inner emotion. This builds to an emotional peak and he freezes. Music stops.

"Pomp and Circumstance" begins again. **Actor 1** breaks freeze, puts hymnal on pulpit and grabs large Bible. He gestures wildly with a look of anger and great intensity. He points at people in the congregation as if preaching to them. He points at the second actor, shakes his fist, then points up as if indicating heaven and freezes. Music stops.

"The Old Rugged Cross" begins to play. **Actor 2** breaks his freeze, continues his former action, then slowly the action subsides. He looks up and smiles, expressing peace and contentment. He rises joyfully as if to leave and freezes. Music stops.

Pantomime: Two Men Went into a Church...   *Dramatic Moments in Worship* [27]

Pantomime

"Pomp and Circumstance" plays. **Actor 1** breaks freeze, moves arrogantly to pulpit, picks up hymnal and Bible. He glares at the second man, and turns to leave in a huff. He takes a few steps and then slows to a jerky walk, music stops, then starts again, then stops *(in rhythm with the man's steps)*. The music stops, the man lets out a gasp, grabs chest and falls to floor, dropping books. In the silence **Actor 2** breaks his freeze, sees the **Actor 1** and moves to him. Gently he reaches down comforting the man and slowly helps him up. As they rise "The Old Rugged Cross" begins to play again. **Actor 1** looks at **Actor 2** in surprise, then slowly kneels before him. **Actor 2** slowly kneels by him and points up. He puts his arm around the shoulders of **Actor 1** and they bow their heads in prayer as the music ends.

Minister or offstage voice: As surely as I live, the Lord says, every knee will bow before me.

© Copyright 2001 LifeWay Press
Adapted from the same piece published in the Summer 2000 issue
of *Church Musician*, LifeWay Christian Resources.

Pantomime

My Gift

The following is a description of a pantomime on four motivations for giving. It is designed to be used immediately before the offering.

Four people walk to the podium, each with a chair. They place the chairs in a straight line and sit. A fifth person *(usher)* walks to the podium with an offering plate. He passes the plate to the first person *(male)*.

This man looks at the plate, looks at the audience and the other characters onstage and proudly pulls his billfold from his pocket, showing it to everyone in the process. He pulls out a large bill, shows it to everyone, and places it in the plate. He starts to pass the plate to the next person, then stops, hands it back to the usher. He then pulls out his billfold again, pulls another large bill out and shows it to everyone, then proudly places it in the plate. As he starts to put the billfold back in his pocket, he stops, pulls out another large bill, shows it to everyone, and then places it in the plate. He holds the plate out to the woman sitting next to him.

The woman looks at the plate, looks at the other people, reaches into her purse and pulls out a coin. She reluctantly places the coin into the plate. She is aware that people are looking at her. Feeling guilty, she reaches into her purse, takes out another coin

Pantomime: My Gift   *Dramatic Moments in Worship* [29]

Pantomime

and places it in the plate. People are still staring at her. She exhibits a feeling of guilt again, reaches into her purse, takes out a third coin and places it in the plate. Then, she takes the plate with one hand and passes it to the person to her right. Just as she passes the plate she takes her free hand, reaches into the plate and grabs a coin back. Then she passes the plate and puts the coin back into her purse.

The third person is a child. She puts the plate in her lap, takes a handkerchief full of coins and dumps all the coins in the plate. Then she puts the handkerchief into the plate too. With a big smile she passes the plate to the man next to her.

The man reaches into his inside coat pocket, takes out an envelope and places it face-down in the plate.

The usher walks to the end of the row and takes the plate from the fourth person. He stretches the plate toward the congregation very slowly. Then, he slowly moves the plate from side to side making eye contact with the audience as he does so. *(As if to say, what is your gift today?)*

© Copyright 2001 LifeWay Press

[30] **Dramatic Moments in Worship**

Pantomime: My Gift

Sketches

Oh, To Be Like Jesus

The following sketch is based on a true story. It is adapted from the musical drama "Bailey King" by Bill Cates and Ev Robertson. Bailey, an older impoverished Mississippi sharecropper is working in the garden behind his shack. It's a hot summer day.

Narrator: Bailey King, a man who lived in absolute poverty most of his life is working in the garden behind his shack. As he ponders the bean vine and how God makes it wrap around the pole he raises his eyes. Down the dusty road in front of his shack a man is walking toward him. He has an enormous load on his back. The man gets to Bailey's house and stops to rest on an old stump across the road. Bailey moves across the road to meet the man.

Bailey: Hello there, warm day isn't it?

Man: Yes suh, warm and dry!

Bailey: Where bouts you headed?

Man: Well, suh, I gots to carry this produce down to Brown's Landing.

Bailey: Brown's Landing! That must be seven or eight miles from here.

Man: Yes suh, ever bit o' that.

Bailey: That's too big a load for any man to carry that distance.

Man: Ain't got no choice – too many mouths to feed.

Bailey: What you needs a wagon.

Man: *(looking up)* Oh, yes suh, a wagon shoh would be nice!

Sketches: Oh, To Be Like Jesus

Sketches

Bailey: I got a wagon! It's behind the house. Why don't you go ahead and take it?

Man: I cain't take yo wagon!

Bailey: You're not taking it, I'm giving it to you. The horse is hitched up close to it.

Man: HOSSE? You cain't give me no hosse. Folks think I stole it!

Bailey: Well, you can't pull a wagon without a horse.

Man: *(looking hard at Bailey)* Suh, yo' givin' me yo' hosse an' wagon?

Bailey: *(smiling)* That's right!

Man: *(tears fill eyes)* I, I, don't know whats to say. Nobody nevuh gave me nuthin befo'!

Bailey: *(reaching to shake the Man's hand)* Say, what'd you say your name was?

Man: Jenkins, suh. Sam Jenkins.

Bailey: Well Sam, if you ever meet a man that needs that wagon mor'n you do, you give it to him and we'll be even.

Man: Oh, yes suh, yes suh, I sho' will.

[32] **Dramatic Moments in Worship**

Sketches: Oh, To Be Like Jesus

Sketches

Narrator: Bailey King and Sam Jenkins, a man he'd never met in his entire life walked arm in arm around the shack and hitched the horse to the wagon. As he drove away he kept waving and hollering, "Thank ya, suh, thank ya. Thank ya, suh, thank ya!" The next morning when Bailey and Lavinia, his wife, got up there was a sack of produce on the front porch. The next morning, another sack. In fact over the next few weeks there was something on their front porch every morning. They had so much stuff they had to give most of it away! Now, the interesting thing about the story of Bailey King and Sam Jenkins is that the horse and wagon Bailey gave Sam was the only one he had ever owned. In fact, Bailey and his wife Lavinia saved over 20 years to purchase it! Oh, to be like Jesus!

Segue into appropriate hymn or song.

© Copyright 2001 LifeWay Press

Sketches

Angels All Around

The following sketch requires an off-stage Voice to represent God.
The actor playing Gabriel should sit in the audience with a lapel mike, if possible.

Voice: Gabriel, Gabriel, Where are you Gabriel?

Gabriel: *(speaking softly)* I'm here Lord, at *(name of church)* watching and listening to the beautiful music.

Voice: I have a job for you.

Gabriel: Can you wait just a minute Lord? You know how special this time of the year is to me. It's Christmas and these people are singing and talking about Jesus, the *Baby* Jesus. You know how I love Christmas music – and these people sing so beautifully. Their church is all decorated and it's well – very special. You know, it all means so much to me! I like to remember the Baby Jesus along with them. He was a beautiful baby, wasn't He Lord? If I *do* say so myself. I had some pretty important work to do with all that, didn't I Lord?

Voice: Yes, Gabriel, but now I have something . . .

Gabriel: In fact, if it hadn't been for me it wouldn't have all happened, would it?

Voice: Gabriel! Believe me, it would have happened!

Gabriel: Ok, ok, but thank you for letting me have a *little* part in it.

Voice: Gabriel, I think you're disturbing the worship of these people!

Sketches

Gabriel: *(softer)* I don't mean to speak so loudly. I just get excited when I think of the manger, Mary and Joseph, the animals, the shepherds, and of course little Jesus! It was perfect Lord, just perfect.

Voice: Good! Now, if you'll listen, I have another assignment for you!

Gabriel: Lord, before you do that, would it be alright if I interrupted this service at *(name of church)* and told them who I really am and the important role I had at Christmas.

Voice: Well, you could, but many of them wouldn't believe you!

Gabriel: Why not?

Voice: Because they don't believe in angels. At least, not modern-day angels.

Gabriel: But we're all around, all the time! Surely *some* of them know it.

Voice: Some of them do.

Gabriel: Then could I speak to them?

Voice: It's not necessary.

Gabriel: But they might really believe in Jesus if I were to speak directly to them.

Voice: I am speaking directly to them.

Voice: Well, yes, I know but . . .

Voice: They have my Son, my only Son, what more can I give?

Gabriel: You're right of course Lord, I didn't mean any disrespect. Just wanted to help out.

Sketches: Angels All Around   *Dramatic Moments in Worship* [35]

Sketches

Voice: The best way you can help out Gabriel is take my next assignment! Now!

Gabriel: Right! I'll be right there. But what about them *(indicating the congregation)*?

Voice: Oh I've given them the most important assignment already!

Gabriel: I know what it is Lord! It's to tell everybody about the Baby Jesus, isn't it!

Voice: That's right!

Gabriel: And His death, burial and resurrection. Right?

Voice: Right!

Gabriel: Gives me chill bumps just thinking about it. And I guess, I kinda started it all with the announcement, didn't I?

Voice: You did *your* part!

Gabriel: And now it's up to all of them to do *their* part. Isn't that right?

Voice: That's right!

Gabriel: Well can I tell them that?

Voice: I think you already have.

Gabriel: Yes, I suppose I have. I'm sorry everyone for interrupting. This time of the year is very, very special to me. I hope it's very special to you. And by the way, you might want to do what God told you is *your* part, because, *we're* everywhere. We're all around you, watching, listening, and waiting!

———

© Copyright 2001 LifeWay Church Resources

Sketches

Cindy's Perfect Christmas

The following sketch can be performed with minimum scenery. A reclining chair is necessary. A Christmas tree with gifts is optional. All other items (window, etc.) can be pantomimed. Hand props including cookies and milk, and presents should be used if possible. The scene begins with Gramps reclined in the easy chair snoring.

Cindy: Gramps, Gramps, wake up, it's snowing!

Gramps: Unhuh, that's nice honey!

Cindy: On Christmas Eve, it's snowing on Christmas Eve!

Gramps: Unhuh, that's real nice!

Cindy: *(dragging him toward window)* Come on Gramps, look, isn't is beautiful?

Gramps: Real pretty. Yep, sure is real pretty!

Cindy: Oh, Gramps, this is going to be the best Christmas ever!

Gramps: Your Nana and I sure want it to be! We're planning some real special things!

Cindy: I wish Mom and Dad were here.

Gramps: Now Cindy, you know all about that and . . . *(phone rings)*

Nana: *(entering)* I'll get it. *(picks up phone)* Hello! Oh, hi Tom, how are you?

Cindy: It's Dad, Gramps!

Nana: We're doing fine. Just a typical Christmas Eve I guess. The snow's nice though. I've got someone here who wants to speak to you! I'll put her right on! *(hands phone to Cindy)*

Sketches: Cindy's Perfect Christmas

Sketches

Cindy: Hi Dad! Yep! Nana's already making her Christmas cookies – I helped cut them out. I love the snow Dad, it's just perfect. *(pause)* I wish you were *here*, Dad. I know, I know, Mom told me about your agreement. I love you too, here's Nana!

Nana: Hello! Yes, I wrapped it. It'll be under the tree in the morning. Tom, I sure wish you'd come by and visit. It would mean so much to Cindy! *(pause)* No, I haven't heard from her. *(pause)* You will! *(nods to Cindy)* That'll be great! We'll have hot cookies and hot chocolate. Be careful in the snow. Alright, goodbye! Well what do you know about that, he's going to come by this evening! I think you have some pull young lady.

Cindy: I knew it! I just knew it! I'm so happy!

Gramps: Well, we better straighten things up around here. *(starts cleaning up, doorbell rings)* Who could that be?

Nana: I'm not expecting anyone!

Gramps: You better let me get it! *(goes to door, opens it)* Ellen!

Cindy: Mom! *(runs to door, hugs her mom as she enters)*

Nana: Ellen, what a pleasant surprise!

Ellen: It's Christmas Eve, Mom. You know I've never missed a Christmas Eve!

Nana: I know, I wasn't expecting you though this time.

Ellen: Cindy, come help me get some more gifts out of the car. *(they exit)*

[38] *Dramatic Moments in Worship*

Sketches: Cindy's Perfect Christmas

Sketches

Gramps: What are you going to do when Tom shows up?

Nana: How do I know? I didn't plan on any of this happening. I guess we'll just take one minute at a time.

Ellen: Phew! It's getting cold out there!

Gramps: They're saying low teens tonight!

Ellen: Well at least we're here all together on Christmas Eve.

Cindy: I'm so glad you came, Mom!

Ellen: Me too, honey! I'm sorry I couldn't come before now, but you know what the judge said.

Cindy: I hate that judge!

Ellen: Your dad and I have an agreement now so we can visit more often.

Cindy: I hate stupid agreements!

Ellen: Now, Cindy, let's not ruin Christmas Eve with all that!

Cindy: Ok, ok, I just think it's all stupid. Why can't our family be together like we used to?

Ellen: You know your dad and I have had some problems!

Cindy: Well, why didn't you solve them?

Ellen: We tried, but we just couldn't!

Cindy: I bet I could solve them! Mr. Edwards on TV said that there's always a solution to every problem – always. I want our family to be together. *(doorbell rings)*

Sketches: Cindy's Perfect Christmas

Sketches

Nana: I better get it. *(goes to door)* Hi, Tom! *(hugs him)* It's good to see you!

Cindy: Daaaaad . . . *(runs and jumps in his arms)*

Dad: Hey, honey bun! How are you? *(stops, sees Ellen, puts Cindy down)* Ellen, I didn't know you were going to be here.

Nana: *(quickly)* We didn't either. She just popped in a few minutes ago.

Gramps: Hey everyone, how about some cookies and hot chocolate?

Nana: Henry, just a minute, let me help you!

(pause)

Cindy: Dad, I got you a special Christmas present. It's in Nana's room. I got one for you too, Mom!

Ellen: Thank you honey, that's very sweet.

Tom: Ah, me too. I can't wait to open it!

Cindy: I'm so glad you're both here. This is going to be the best Christmas ever!

Tom: Cindy, I think I better be going, I didn't know your mom was going to be here.

Cindy: Dad, don't go, please stay! Please?

Ellen: No, Tom, you go ahead and stay, I'll go. Cindy thanks for helping me get the gifts in and . . .

Cindy: Mom, don't go. It's ok if you both stay. I promise not to tell the judge. It's Christmas and I want you to be with me at Christmas, please? Please?

Sketches

Ellen: *(stops at door, looks at Tom, he shrugs shoulders, looks at Cindy)* Ok. For a little while anyway.

Nana: *(entering with Gramps)* Hot cookies and hot chocolate for everyone!

Cindy: Yummmy! I love Nana's cookies.

Ellen: Sure does smell nice, Mom. I remember that smell so well.

Tom: Ahh, yeah! Your cookies are always the best.

Nana: Well, I hope you enjoy them. I can't tell you how nice it is having all our family together.

Cindy: Nana, Mom and Dad promised not to go! I made them. I told them I wouldn't tell the judge. Isn't that great?

Gramps: I say what the judge doesn't know won't hurt him! *(chuckles)*

Nana: What's that Henry?

Gramps: Oh nothing, nothing, just talking to myself!

Cindy: Hey! We didn't pray before eating the cookies! Gramps . . .

Gramps: Ah, yeah, that's right.

Cindy: Ok, everyone in a circle and take hands. *(Cindy stands between Tom and Ellen)*

Gramps: Cindy, why don't you pray. You're about as happy as anybody here tonight.

Cindy: Dear God, thank you for the delicious cookies and hot chocolate. And thank you God for letting our family be all together tonight. And dear God, if it's not

Sketches: Cindy's Perfect Christmas

Sketches

too much, would you fix it with the judge so Mom and Dad can come home with me all the time? Please, God? Amen.

Tom: Cindy, I don't think you should ask God for that, it's just not possible!

Nana: Ah, Henry, I need to check on something in the kitchen. Can you help me?

Gramps: Sure, of course.

Cindy: Mr. Rogers says anything is possible. And if Mr. Rogers *says* it, I know God can *do* it.

Ellen: Well, honey. It's not as simple as that. You see, your dad and I have an agreement.

Cindy: I don't care about your ol' agreement. All I know is that we're a family, and families are suppose to be together! I want us to be

together! Please???? *(awkward pause)*

Ellen: Cindy, please don't ask . . .

Tom: Cindy, I know it means a lot to you, but . . .

Cindy: Ok, Dad, who's more important here? Me, or you and Mom?

Tom: Why you are honey, you know I love you.

Ellen: Well of course we love you dear, we're your parents.

Cindy: Then if I'm so important, why can't our family be together?

Ellen: Well you see . . .

Tom: Things happen and, well . . .

Cindy: Mr. Rogers says people let you know what's important to them by what they do, not what

[42] *Dramatic Moments in Worship*

Sketches: Cindy's Perfect Christmas

Sketches

they say. You say you love me. I guess the only way I'll ever know that's true is if our family's back together again.

Ellen: *(tearing up)* Cindy, you know I love you!

Cindy: Then show it!

Ellen: *(starting to cry)* It's all so hard honey, so hard!

Tom: Now don't start crying Ellen, you know I can't handle that.

Ellen: I'm sorry, I'll try not to. . .

Cindy: Do you love me, Dad?

Tom: Of course, of course!

Cindy: Then show it!

Tom: I, I... *(stops, looks at Cindy, looks at Ellen, pauses)*

Cindy: Well, will you at least talk about it? Without that old judge?

Ellen: I suppose we could talk . . .

Tom: Sure, if it'll make you happy, Cindy.

Cindy: Yeaaaaa! *(yells)* Nana, Gramps come on, let's open the presents. *(Nana and Gramps enter)* Mom and Dad have promised to talk about our family being together again. Isn't that great!

Nana: That's wonderful, Cindy!

Gramps: Sounds pretty good to me!

Cindy: See, I told you Gramps! This is going to be the best Christmas ever!

© Copyright 2001 LifeWay Press

Sketches: Cindy's Perfect Christmas

Sketches

Family War

The following sketch is designed to be used as a sermon introduction or illustration. Al enters, sets down briefcase or lunch box, takes off coat, throws it over a chair. Opens newspaper, sits exhausted in chair and begins reading paper.

Off-stage sound of garage door opening, car entering and engine cutting off. Door opens and closes. Woman enters with two bags of groceries.

Susan: Al, will you help me get the rest of the groceries. I've got several bags, the pantry is really depleted.

Al: In a minute. *(pause, Susan puts bags on table)*

Susan: I've got ice cream Al. Will you help me now?

Al: I just got in. I'm exhausted. Give me minute. *(continues reading paper)*

Susan: *(starts for door, stops, turns)* Why do you always do this?

Al: Hmmmm?

Susan: You never help me when I need you!

Al: *(still reading)* Hmmmm?

Susan: *(louder)* I said, you never help me when I really need you!

Al: Ok, ok, I heard you the first time.

Susan: Then why are you still sitting there?

Al: I just told you, I'm exhausted, I had a rough day. I'll be with you in a minute.

Sketches

Susan: I need you *now*!

Al: I'm not coming NOW!

Susan: Oh, I know that. You won't be coming by next Christmas!

Al: That's right, keep it up and you'll be carrying in *all* the groceries.

Susan: *(looks in trash basket)* Oh, you got *that* right. I see the trash is still here from two days ago.

Al: *(no response)*

Susan: *(louder)* I said the trash is still here from *two days ago*.

Al: *(no response)*

Susan: *(walks over to him, jerks paper from his hands)* Why do you treat me like this?

Al: *(grabs paper back, no response)*

Susan: *(grabs paper and takes it away to table)* I'm sick and tired of being treated like this. Get your lazy self up and help me with the groceries!

Al: *(jumps up, follows her, turns her around grabs paper)* Don't *ever* grab the paper when I'm reading it!

Susan: Why not? It's the only way I can get your attention.

Al: You do it again and it'll be the last time.

Susan: I wouldn't have to grab it if you'd help out!

Al: I'll help out when I'm ready!

Susan: I – need – you – *now*!

Al: You already said that.

Susan: I'm saying it *again*!

Sketches: Family War

Dramatic Moments in Worship [45]

Sketches

Al: In a minute!

Susan: Now!

Al: I don't take orders!

Susan: You're sooo lazy!

Al: *(throws paper down)* That does it!

Susan: Good!

Al: I've had it with you!

Susan: Ditto!

Al: *(yelling)* Shut up!

Susan: *(yelling)* Never!

(they freeze)

© Copyright 2001 LifeWay Press

Call to Worship

Sing to the Lord

Psalm 98: 1-6 *(NIV)*

A Call to Worship for five voices. To be spoken dramatically with background music.
A drum roll, tympani or other acoustic instrument can be added.
Follow the piece immediately with a hymn/song of celebration.

1: Sing

2 & 3: Sing

All: Sing to the Lord a new song!

4: For He has done marvelous things!

5: He has made His salvation known!

1: And revealed His righteousness to the nations!

2: He has remembered His love

2 & 3: And His faithfulness to the house of Israel!

4: All the ends of the earth

4 & 5: Have seen the salvation of our God.

All: Shout for joy to the Lord, all the earth!

1 & 2: Burst into jubilant song with music!

3 & 4: Make music to the Lord with the harp!

5: With the harp and sounds of singing,

1: With trumpets

1 & 2: And the blast of the ram's horn!

3: Shout

4: Shout for joy!

All: Shout for joy before the Lord, the King!

© Copyright 2001 LifeWay Press

Call to Worship

Light in the Darkness

Genesis 1; John 1 *(NIV)*

Three readers may be close together or scattered: on the podium, spread in the congregation or even in the balcony! They read very dramatically with steady progression and build to the final line. Background sound is recommended. This might include a tympani or perhaps the organist holding down a low pedal note on the organ.

Voice 1: In the beginning

Voice 2: In the beginning, God

Voice 3: In the beginning, God created

Voice 1: In the beginning was the Word

Voice 2: And the Word was with God

Voice 3: And the Word was God

Voice 1 & 2: In Him was Life

Voice 3: And His Life was the Light of Men

Voice 1 & 2: His Light shines in the darkness

All Voices: And the darkness can never conquer it.

Follow this immediately with prayer or hymn of celebration.

———

© Copyright 2001 LifeWay Press

Call to Worship

We Are His

Psalm 95: 1-7 *(NIV)*

The following selection calls for five voices – three men and two women, or two men and three women. Begin with a drum roll or possibly brief trumpet fanfare.

Voice 1: Come,

Voices 2 & 3: Let us sing for joy to the Lord;

All: Let us shout aloud to the Rock of our salvation.

Voice 4: Let us come before him with thanksgiving

Voice 5: And extol him with music and song.

Voices 1 & 2: For the Lord is the great God,

Voices 3 & 4: the great King above all gods.

Voice 1: In his hand are the depths of the earth,

Voice 2: And the mountain peaks belong to him.

Voice 3: The sea is his, for he made it,

Voice 4: And his hands formed the dry land.

Voice 1: Come,

Voices 2 & 3: let us bow down in worship,

Voices 4 & 5: Let us kneel before the Lord our Maker;

Voice 1: For he is our God and we are the people of his pasture,

Voice 5: The flock under his care.

Voice 1: So come,

Voices 2 & 3: let us sing for joy to the Lord;

Voices 3 & 4: Let us shout aloud

All: to the Rock of our salvation

© Copyright 2001 LifeWay Press

Call to Worship: We Are His

Dramatic Moments in Worship [49]

Audience Participation

When God Calls

The following sketch is ideal for a youth rally, or youth worship time. It is performed as a rap with snapping fingers or perhaps drums accompanying it. The congregation is divided into four groups. *Group 1* reacts to, "Moses." They stand, throw their arms out and shake them to represent a burning bush. The *Group 2* reacts to "Jonah." They stand bend their knees, let out a loud "burp." At the same time they move their arms from their stomachs to their mouths and then out to suggest whale throwing Jonah onto the shore. The *Group 3* reacts to "Mary." They stand, put hands together to the right of their faces, lean head on hands as if sleeping, yawn, and then on cue jerk upright, throw hands straight into the air and speak loudly, "Go." The *group 4* reacts to "Paul." They stand, turn around 360 degrees, then throw their arms and hands up as if to be protected from an intense light. On the word, "Go," they break freeze and point right arm and forefinger out 45 degrees up and forward. The Leader speaks the following and the congregation responds. He speaks a line, then they speak a line and carry out the appropriate action. The entire congregation speaks the final, "When God calls I'll go!"

Leader: God's calls us to be His people! When God calls I'll go!

Congregation: God's calls us to be His people! When God calls I'll go!

Leader: *(repeats, raising pitch, volume and intensity)* God's calls us to be His people! When God calls I'll go!

Congregation: God's calls us to be His people! When God calls I'll go!

Leader: God called Moses at a burning bush! When God calls I'll go!

Group 1: God called Moses at a burning bush! When God calls I'll go! Hey!

Leader: God called Jonah in the belly of a fish! When God calls I'll go!

Audience Participation

Group 2: God called Jonah in the belly of a fish! When God calls I'll go! Burp!

Leader: God called Mary in the middle of the night! When God calls I'll go!

Group 3: God called Mary in the middle of the night! When God calls I'll go! Go!

Leader: God called Paul on the road to Damascus! When God calls I'll go!

Group 4: God called Paul on the road to Damascus! When God calls I'll go! Yo!

Leader: God's called us to be His People! When God calls I'll go!

Congregation: God's called us to be His People! When God calls I'll go!

Leader: God called Moses at a burning bush!

Group 1: When God calls I'll go! Hey!

Leader: God called Jonah in the belly of a fish!

Group 2: When God calls I'll go! Burp!

Leader: God called Mary in the middle of the night!

Group 3: When God calls I'll go! Go!

Leader: God called Paul on the road to Damascus!

Group 4: When God calls I'll go! Yo!

Leader: God calls us to be His People! When God calls I'll go!

All: God calls us to be His People! When God calls I'll go!

© Copyright 2001 LifeWay Press

Scenarios

The Game of Life

The following material describes a dramatic scene. The actors take this material, improvise with it and develop their own script.

Two characters, father & son

A father and son are sitting side by side, watching a baseball game.

They are eating peanuts and each has a large drink.

They are talking about the game, best players, etc.

During their conversation they begin to talk about the large salaries of the players, fancy cars, etc.

The father begins to talk about what's really important in life.

They discuss family, personal happiness, and of course the Lord.

The father explains that being saved and having the Lord in our hearts is more valuable than all the money in the world.

Scenarios

A Christian Responsibility

The following material describes a dramatic scene. The actors take this material, improvise with it and develop their own script.

Two characters, both women

Two women are sitting at a table during coffee break at work.

They are discussing items of personal interest and also talk about the boss, sorry working conditions, and co-workers.

One of the women wants to know if the other has heard about the affair going on between the boss and his secretary.

The other woman has not heard about it.

During the discussion the second woman finally tells the other woman not to mention the affair unless she can prove it's going on.

Since the boss and his secretary are Christians she tells her it's their responsibility to first go together and speak to each of them about the affair.

She lets her know it is important to do everything possible to try and help the boss and his secretary.

They end the scene by praying together to be more effective as Christians. Instead of gossiping – to go and do something about the situation.

Scenarios: A Christian Responsibility

Scenarios

True Love Waits

The following material describes a dramatic scene. The actors take this material, improvise with it and develop their own script.

Two characters, both women

Two young women are discussing their career goals.

During the discussion they talk about where they'd like to live, types of houses, income, etc.

Finally they get around to families, number of children, etc.

And then who they'd like to marry.

Each wants a Christian husband.

They describe personal traits they'd like to see in their husbands.

One of the girls wants to know if the other wants her husband to be a virgin.

She then shares why she's protected her virginity so she can share that with her husband as God intended.

Scenarios

The Lord's Prayer

The following scenario is based on a sketch by Clyde Lee Herring in a book, *If God Talked Out Loud* published by Broadman Press. The book has been out of print for several years. However, it is easy to take the basic idea and improvise your own script.

An actor stands up and begins the Lord's Prayer.

At the end of each phrase an offstage voice interrupts.

The voice represents God.

The actor is questioned about each part of the prayer.

What does it mean? Why is it said? How does it effect us?

The resulting dialogue can be delightful and funny, but very insightful and educational.

The actor begins to understand what it all really means.

He concludes by making a commitment not to pray words unless he's sure of their meaning and can make it personal.

Scenarios: The Lord's Prayer

Scenarios

Worship Changes

The following material describes a dramatic scene. The actors take this material, improvise with it and develop their own script.

Two characters, husband & wife

A husband and wife are driving home from church.

They are discussing parts of the worship service. The wife likes the music. The husband finds it all boring.

He admits having trouble staying awake.

They concur on some common themes: the sermon's too long, there's not enough variety in the music, there's not enough congregational involvement, some people don't dress appropriately, etc.

Finally the wife asks the husband what he would do if he could change it.

They have trouble coming up with elements both can agree on.

Eventually they admit that the problem may not be the sermon or the music, but the worshippers.

Do people attend expecting to meet God? Do they seek Him throughout the service?

Do they look for His words of encouragement to them through the sermon, music and other elements?

They end by agreeing to attend church next Sunday with a different attitude.

[56] Dramatic Moments in Worship   *Scenarios: Worship Changes*

Scenarios

Prepare to Worship

The following material describes a dramatic scene. The actors take this material, improvise with it and develop their own script.

Two women choir members in robes are sitting side by side on the podium facing the audience.

The choir has just entered – the women begin talking as the service is about to begin.

They comment on the terrible weather, poor choir attendance, and a terrible music special they anticipate.

It'll be bad because the soprano soloists "warbles."

They also comment on people in the congregation.

They can't believe some people are present because they were out drinking the night before.

They notice that some people are so busy talking they don't even realize the choir has entered and the service is about to begin.

One of them finally comments she thought Christians were supposed to prepare spiritually for worship to meet God.

The other lady ends the scene by asking, "Does that include the choir?"

Scenarios: Prepare to Worship

Scenarios

Offering Interrupted

The following material describes a dramatic scene. The actors take this material, improvise with it and develop their own script.

The offertory hymn and prayer are over.

The ushers are about to pass the plates when a person stands up in the congregation and asks them to stop.

He apologizes for interrupting, but shares with the congregation a deep concern about their own personal attitudes toward the offering.

He wonders how many people in the congregation came prepared to make a sacrificial gift.

How many are even thinking about giving while the plates are being passed?

How many actually prepared to give before coming to church?

He wonders if people are praying for God to bless their offering?

Are they praying that the gifts will be used effectively, etc.?

Finally, he asks that the ushers pause for a moment until everyone in the congregation has a moment to consider their gifts!

He might conclude with a brief prayer asking God to prepare each member for the gift they are about to give.

[58] *Dramatic Moments in Worship*   *Scenarios: Offering Interrupted*

Scenarios

Hymn Interruption

The following material describes a dramatic scene. The actors take this material, improvise with it and develop their own script.

The music director announces a hymn/song number to the congregation, and before he can begin directing, a person in the congregation stands and asks why they are singing that hymn.

This person may dialogue briefly with the music director about the hymn.

During this dialogue the music director discusses the true meaning of the hymn/song.

He might even ask for personal testimonies from people in the congregation/choir *(pre-assigned)* related to the meaning of the hymn.

The scene concludes with the director asking the congregation to sing the hymn/song with the conviction of its meaning.

Scenarios: Hymn Interruption   *Dramatic Moments in Worship* [59]

Scenarios

Sermon Interruption

The following material describes a dramatic scene. The actors take this material, improvise with it and develop their own script.

The pastor works with one or more people in the congregation on one or more questions to be raised during the sermon.

The pastor begins preaching in his traditional manner.

At a key moment in the sermon, someone in the congregation stands and asks a question related to the theme of the message.

Often the best questions are those which relate to personal application of the message.

These allow the pastor to easily answer with specific suggestions for implementing the message.

The pastor can later relate to this questioning as a good example of what we need to be asking God.

Do we sincerely seek His will in the sermon?

Do we pray for specific personal help in the sermon and look/listen for it?

Do we make notes that we can use later in our personal devotion time, etc.?

Scenarios

On Mission

The following material describes a dramatic scene. The actors take this material, improvise with it and develop their own script.

Two people meet on the podium.

One is asking **Two** for a gift to assist in **One's** mission project. **One** is going with a church group to a foreign country for a one or two week trip. **Two** asks why he should give money so someone can take what appears to be a vacation with the word "mission" attached to it.

One explains what the group hopes to accomplish on the trip, and discusses their busy daily schedule. **Two** suggests that full-time missionaries could do all of that much better.

One, near tears, begins to explain how God spoke to her personally about making a personal financial sacrifice and gift of vacation time for the work. **One** shares the vision God has given her about people in real need and shares a personal desire to help. **Two** comments that there are so many needs at home. Why not use the resources here?

One then asks **Two** how he would suggest using the money at home. Ideas emerge.

One asks the **Two** if he feels a calling to those local mission needs. **One** then agrees to give all that he can to **Two** for those local needs. **One** also commits to work with and support the local needs as much, if not more than the foreign need. They end by excitedly discussing all the possibilities in service of the Lord!

Scenarios: On Mission   *Dramatic Moments in Worship* [61]

Children Sermon Scenarios

The following material describes dramatic scenes.
The actors take this material, improvise with it and develop their own scripts.

Our Heavenly Father

An actor enters in biblical costume explaining that he is the prodigal son's father. He asks the children if they know who the prodigal son is. Then he briefly reviews the story. Finally he tells them that the love he has for his son is similar to the love that God has for us. He encourages the children to know that God always loves them, although He may not love their sin, and that He is always waiting with His arms open to forgive and forget.

The Missionaries

Two actors enter in biblical costume. They are portraying Paul and Barnabas. They discuss their travels and what it means to be a missionary. They ask if the children are aware that all of us are missionaries. They explain what it means to be ambassadors for Christ. They conclude by encouraging the children to be missionaries at home, at school, and wherever they go.

A Wicked Tongue

Two puppets appear. One is crying and the other wants to know why. The crying puppet shares some of the terrible things others are saying about him. He talks about the fact they're not true, but more importantly, how they hurt him. The other puppet consoles him and interacts with the children. He asks the children if they like to hurt people. He shows the children how untrue things said about another person can hurt that person.

[62] Dramatic Moments in Worship

Children Sermon Scenarios

Scripture Index

Gen. 1—
Light in the
Darkness

Lev. 19:18—
Oh, To Be Like
Jesus

Deut. 6:5—
The Game of Life

Ex. 3—
When God Calls

Jonah 3: 1-10—
When God Calls

Ps. 95:1-7—
We Are His

Ps. 95:6—
Prepare to Worship

Ps. 98:1-6—
Sing to the Lord

Mal. 3:10—
My Gift

Matt. 2:6—
The Shepherd

Matt. 6:9-13—
The Lord's Prayer

Matt. 6:25-34—
Oh, To Be Like
Jesus

Matt. 8:1-3—
God's Amazing
Healing Grace
(The Leper)

Matt. 9: 36—
The Shepherd

Matt. 27-28—The
Parable of the Wood

Mark 6:34—
The Shepherd

Luke 1: 26-28—
When God Calls

Luke 5:12—God's
Amazing Healing
Grace (The Leper)

Luke 15:11-32—
Our Heavenly
Father

Luke 17:11-19—
God's Amazing
Grace (The Leper)

Luke 18:9-14—
Two Men Went into
a Church

Luke 19—
Redeemed
(Zacchaeus)

John 1—
Light in the
Darkness

John 4:1-26—
My Wonderful
Peace (The Woman
at the Well)

John 4:23—
Worship Changes;
The Visitor

John 7:36-50—
Forgiven

John 8:43—
Sermon
Interruption

John 10:1-18—
The Shepherd

John 13:13-17,
34-35—Oh, To Be
Like Jesus

John 15:12—
Oh, To Be Like
Jesus

Acts 9: 2-8—
When God Calls

Rom. 14:10-13—
A Christian
Responsibility

1 Cor. 2:2-5—
The Parable of the
Wood

1 Cor. 2:6-16—
The Christmas Gift

1 Cor. 14:15—
Hymn Interruption

1 Cor. 14:24-25—
The Visitor

2 Cor. 5: 16-19—
Cindy's Perfect
Christmas

2 Cor. 5:20—
On Mission

2 Cor. 9:6-7, 11—
My Gift

2 Cor. 9: 6-8—
Offering
Interruption

2 Cor. 13:4-5—
The Parable of the
Wood

Eph. 5:5—
True Love Waits

Heb. 13:1-2—
Angels All Around

Heb. 13:4—
True Love Waits

James 1:26—
A Wicked Tongue

James 3:6, 8—
A Wicked Tongue

Rev. 14:6-7—
The Parable of the
Wood

Topical Index

Angels:
Angels All Around

Call (to ministry):
When God Calls
I'll Go

Celebration:
Sing to the Lord;
We Are His

Christmas:
The Christmas
Gift; The Parable
of the Wood; Angels
All Around; Cindy's
Perfect Christmas

**Church Atten-
dance:** The Visitor

Creation: Light in
the Darkness; The
Parable of the Wood

Crucifixion: The
Parable of the Wood

Darkness: Light
in the Darkness

**Divorce (separa-
tion):** Cindy's
Perfect Christmas

Easter:
The Parable of the
Wood

Family:
The Game of Life;
Cindy's Perfect
Christmas; Our
Heavenly Father

Father's Day:
The Game of Life

Forgiveness:
A Christian
Responsibility

**Giving
(sacrificial):**
Oh, To Be
Like Jesus; The
Christmas Gift

Giving (offering):
My Gift

Gossip:
A Wicked Tongue

Grace:
God's Amazing
Healing Grace; My
Wonderful Peace;
Redeemed; Forgiven

**Healing
(Physical):**
God's Amazing
Healing Grace;
The Shepherd

**Healing
(Spiritual):**
My Wonderful
Peace; Forgiven;
Our Heavenly
Father; Redeemed

Leper:
God's Amazing
Healing Grace

Light: Light in
the Darkness

Ministry: A Chris-
tian Responsibility;
A Wicked Tongue

Missions:
The Missionaries;
On Mission

Neighbor:
Oh, To Be Like Jesus

Offering:
My Gift; Offering
Interruption

Parable:
The Parable of
the Wood; Two
Men Went into
a Church; Our
Heavenly Father

Prayer:
The Lord's Prayer;
Two Men Went into
a Church

Puppets:
A Wicked Tongue

Reconciliation:
Cindy's Perfect
Christmas; My
Wonderful Peace;
Redeemed;
Forgiven

Salvation:
God's Amazing
Healing Grace; My
Wonderful Peace;
Redeemed

Sermon: Sermon
Interruption

Sexual Purity
True Love Waits

Shepherd:
The Shepherd

Sin: A Wicked
Tongue; A Chris-
tian Responsibility;
Forgiven

Singing (Song):
Sing to the Lord

**Samaritan
Woman:** My
Wonderful Peace

Witnessing:
God's Amazing
Healing Grace;
My Wonderful
Peace; The Visitor

Worship:
Worship Changes;
The Lord's Prayer;
The Visitor; Two
Men Went into a
Church; My Gift;
Prepare to Worship;
Offering Interrup-
tion; Sermon Inter-
ruption

Youth: True Love
Waits; When God
Calls I'll Go